Die Fliegenden Süßigkeiten Der Whizzpop Lane: Zweisprachige Englisch-Deutsche Geschichten

My Pommeline

Published by My Pommeline, 2024.

While every precaution has been taken in the preparation of this book, the publisher assumes no responsibility for errors or omissions, or for damages resulting from the use of the information contained herein.

DIE FLIEGENDEN SÜSSIGKEITEN DER WHIZZPOP LANE: ZWEISPRACHIGE ENGLISCH-DEUTSCHE GESCHICHTEN

First edition. October 28, 2024.

ISBN: 979-8227949103

Written by My Pommeline.

Table of Contents

Tilly and the Talking Trees 1

Tilly und die sprechenden Bäume 7

The Enormous Elephant Surprise 13

Die Enorme Elefantenüberraschung................................19

Mr. Bumble's Strange Invention..25

Mr. Bumbles seltsame Erfindung 33

The Misbehaving Magic Paintbrush 41

Der Ungezogene Magische Pinsel 47

The Flying Sweets of Whizzpop Lane 53

Die fliegenden Süßigkeiten der Whizzpop Lane 59

Tilly and the Talking Trees

Once upon a time, in a small village tucked between rolling hills and golden fields, there lived a curious little girl named Tilly. Tilly had a great love for nature, especially the woods at the edge of her village. Every day after school, she would wander into the forest, exploring its mossy paths and listening to the wind rustling through the leaves.

One warm afternoon, Tilly discovered something extraordinary. As she wandered deeper into the forest, she came across a clearing where the trees were unlike any she had seen before. Their bark was smoother, their leaves seemed to shimmer, and as Tilly walked closer, she heard something that made her stop in her tracks—a soft whisper.

"Hello," a voice said.

Tilly looked around, puzzled. "Who's there?"

"It's me," the voice replied, and to Tilly's amazement, the words came from a tall, grand oak tree standing proudly in the middle of the clearing.

"Did you just... talk?" Tilly asked, her eyes wide with wonder.

"Yes, indeed," the oak replied in a deep, gentle voice. "Welcome to the heart of the Talking Trees."

Tilly's jaw dropped as, one by one, the other trees began to chime in, introducing themselves in voices of all tones and pitches. Some were high and giggly, like the young saplings, while others, like the ancient yews, spoke slowly and wisely.

"I'm Oakley, the oldest tree in this forest," said the grand oak. "We've been waiting for someone like you, Tilly."

"How do you know my name?" Tilly asked, stepping closer.

"We know all about you," said a tall birch with silvery bark. "We've seen you wandering through the forest, taking care not to disturb us."

"The forest speaks to those who listen," added a delicate willow, its branches swaying gently as if in a silent dance.

Tilly was amazed. She had always known there was something special about the woods, but she never imagined the trees could talk!

Oakley bent a low branch toward her. "We have something to show you," he said.

With that, the trees began to sing—a song so beautiful it made the birds stop to listen. As they sang, the trees swayed and danced, their branches waving in rhythm. Flowers bloomed at their roots, and the leaves shimmered in every shade of green and gold.

Tilly giggled and clapped her hands. "This is amazing! I'll come here every day!"

But just as the last note of the song faded into the breeze, the mood in the forest changed. The trees' leaves drooped, and their branches stopped swaying.

"What's wrong?" Tilly asked.

"We're in danger," said Oakley solemnly. "Humans plan to cut us down."

Tilly gasped. "Cut you down? Why?"

"They want to build roads and houses where we stand," said a small fir tree, its voice quivering. "They don't understand how special this forest is."

Tilly frowned. She couldn't let that happen. The Talking Trees were her friends now, and she had to do something to save them. But what?

Oakley gave her a wise look. "We've seen your love for stories and rhyme, Tilly. Perhaps that's where the solution lies."

Tilly's eyes lit up. Of course! She would use a rhyme—a magical one that would help her save the forest.

That night, Tilly stayed up late in her room, her head buzzing with words and ideas. She thought about the trees, their song, and the way they danced in the breeze. She knew she had to come up with the perfect rhyme, one that would show everyone just how important the forest was.

The next morning, Tilly marched into the village square, where the developers were setting up plans to clear the forest. A crowd had gathered to watch.

With her heart pounding, Tilly stepped forward and began to speak:

"Listen close, and hear my plea,

The forest's voice belongs to thee.

These trees, they sing, they dance, they play,

They must not fall, they're here to stay.

For in their roots and in their leaves,

Are stories spun by gentle breeze.

Their branches sway, their whispers sing,

Of magic born in every ring.

So builders, please, I ask of you,

Let nature's beauty shine on through.

This forest's heart must not be stilled,

Let it remain—let dreams be filled."

As Tilly finished, the crowd was silent. The developers looked at each other, unsure of what to say. Just then, a soft breeze blew through the square, and for a brief moment, it sounded like the trees themselves were whispering Tilly's rhyme.

The head developer, a tall man with a clipboard, cleared his throat. "Well," he said slowly, "I hadn't thought of the forest in that way."

"Neither did I," said a woman in the crowd. "We should protect the trees."

One by one, the villagers began to agree. Soon, the developer nodded. "Alright, we'll find another place for our project. The forest will stay."

Tilly beamed, her heart swelling with pride. She had done it! The Talking Trees were safe.

That afternoon, she returned to the magical clearing. Oakley and the other trees greeted her with a song, their voices filled with gratitude.

"Thank you, Tilly," Oakley said. "You saved us."

Tilly smiled and sat beneath Oakley's wide branches, feeling the warmth of the sun and the gentle rustle of leaves all around her. "I didn't do it alone," she said. "We did it together."

And from that day on, Tilly visited the Talking Trees often, where they sang and danced and told stories. The forest remained a magical place, protected and cherished, thanks to a brave little girl and the power of rhyme.

Tilly und die sprechenden Bäume

Es war einmal in einem kleinen Dorf, das zwischen sanften Hügeln und goldenen Feldern lag, ein neugieriges kleines Mädchen namens Tilly. Tilly hatte eine große Liebe zur Natur, besonders zu den Wäldern am Rand ihres Dorfes. Jeden Tag nach der Schule wanderte sie in den Wald, erkundete die moosbedeckten Pfade und hörte dem Wind zu, der durch die Blätter rauschte.

Eines warmen Nachmittags entdeckte Tilly etwas Außergewöhnliches. Als sie tiefer in den Wald wanderte, stieß sie auf eine Lichtung, wo die Bäume anders waren als alle, die sie zuvor gesehen hatte. Ihre Rinde war glatter, ihre Blätter schienen zu schimmern, und als Tilly näher kam, hörte sie etwas, das sie zum Stehenbleiben brachte – ein sanftes Flüstern.

„Hallo", sagte eine Stimme.

Tilly schaute sich um, verwirrt. „Wer ist da?"

„Ich bin es", antwortete die Stimme, und zu Tillys Erstaunen kamen die Worte von einer hohen, prächtigen Eiche, die stolz in der Mitte der Lichtung stand.

„Hast du gerade... gesprochen?" fragte Tilly, ihre Augen weit vor Staunen.

„Ja, in der Tat", antwortete die Eiche mit einer tiefen, sanften Stimme. „Willkommen im Herzen der sprechenden Bäume."

Tillys Kinn klappte herunter, als einer nach dem anderen die anderen Bäume zu sprechen begannen und sich mit Stimmen aller Töne und Tonlagen vorstellten. Einige waren hoch und kichernd, wie die jungen Setzlinge, während andere, wie die alten Eiben, langsam und weise sprachen.

„Ich bin Oakley, der älteste Baum in diesem Wald", sagte die große Eiche. „Wir haben auf jemanden wie dich gewartet, Tilly."

„Wie kennst du meinen Namen?" fragte Tilly, die näher trat.

„Wir wissen alles über dich", sagte eine hohe Birke mit silberner Rinde. „Wir haben dich durch den Wald wandern sehen, darauf bedacht, uns nicht zu stören."

„Der Wald spricht zu denen, die zuhören", fügte eine zarte Weide hinzu, deren Äste sanft wie in einem stillen Tanz schwankten.

Tilly war erstaunt. Sie hatte schon immer gewusst, dass es etwas Besonderes an den Wäldern gab, aber sie hätte nie gedacht, dass die Bäume sprechen könnten!

Oakley beugte einen niedrigen Ast zu ihr. „Wir haben dir etwas zu zeigen", sagte er.

Damit begannen die Bäume zu singen – ein Lied so schön, dass die Vögel inne hielten, um zuzuhören. Während sie sangen, schwankten und tanzten die Bäume, ihre Äste bewegten sich im Rhythmus. Blumen blühten an ihren Wurzeln, und die Blätter schimmerten in allen Grüntönen und Gold.

Tilly kicherte und klatschte in die Hände. „Das ist erstaunlich! Ich werde jeden Tag hierher kommen!"

Doch gerade als der letzte Ton des Liedes in die Brise verklang, änderte sich die Stimmung im Wald. Die Blätter der Bäume hingen herab, und ihre Äste hörten auf zu schwingen.

„Was ist los?" fragte Tilly.

„Wir sind in Gefahr", sagte Oakley ernst. „Die Menschen planen, uns abzuholzen."

Tilly schnappte nach Luft. „Euch abholzen? Warum?"

„Sie wollen Straßen und Häuser dort bauen, wo wir stehen", sagte ein kleiner Tannenbaum, dessen Stimme zitterte. „Sie verstehen nicht, wie besonders dieser Wald ist."

Tilly runzelte die Stirn. Sie konnte das nicht zulassen. Die sprechenden Bäume waren jetzt ihre Freunde, und sie musste etwas tun, um sie zu retten. Aber was?

Oakley warf ihr einen weisen Blick zu. „Wir haben deine Liebe zu Geschichten und Reimen gesehen, Tilly. Vielleicht liegt die Lösung darin."

Tillys Augen leuchteten auf. Natürlich! Sie würde ein Reim benutzen – einen magischen, der ihr helfen würde, den Wald zu retten.

In dieser Nacht blieb Tilly spät in ihrem Zimmer wach, ihr Kopf summte vor Worten und Ideen. Sie dachte an die Bäume, ihr Lied und die Art, wie sie im Wind tanzten. Sie wusste, dass sie den perfekten Reim finden musste, um allen zu zeigen, wie wichtig der Wald war.

Am nächsten Morgen marschierte Tilly auf den Dorfplatz, wo die Entwickler Pläne machten, um den Wald abzuholzen. Eine Menge hatte sich versammelt, um zuzusehen.

Mit klopfendem Herzen trat Tilly vor und begann zu sprechen:

„Hört gut zu und hört mein Flehen,

Die Stimme des Waldes gehört zu euch.

Diese Bäume, sie singen, sie tanzen, sie spielen,

Sie dürfen nicht fallen, sie sind hier zu bleiben.

Denn in ihren Wurzeln und in ihren Blättern,

Sind Geschichten gesponnen vom sanften Wind.

Ihre Äste schwanken, ihre Flüstern singen,

Von Magie geboren in jedem Ring.

Also, Bauherren, bitte, ich bitte euch,

Lasst die Schönheit der Natur weiter scheinen.

Das Herz dieses Waldes darf nicht stillstehen,

Lasst es bestehen – lasst Träume erblühen."

Als Tilly fertig war, herrschte im Publikum Stille. Die Entwickler schauten sich unsicher an. Just in dem Moment wehte eine sanfte Brise durch den Platz, und für einen kurzen Moment klang es, als würden die Bäume selbst Tillys Reim flüstern.

Der leitende Entwickler, ein großer Mann mit einem Klemmbrett, räusperte sich. „Nun," sagte er langsam, „ich hatte den Wald nicht auf diese Weise betrachtet."

„Ich auch nicht," sagte eine Frau in der Menge. „Wir sollten die Bäume schützen."

Einer nach dem anderen begannen die Dorfbewohner zuzustimmen. Bald nickte der Entwickler. „In Ordnung, wir werden einen anderen Platz für unser Projekt finden. Der Wald bleibt."

Tilly strahlte, ihr Herz war voller Stolz. Sie hatte es geschafft! Die sprechenden Bäume waren in Sicherheit.

An diesem Nachmittag kehrte sie zur magischen Lichtung zurück. Oakley und die anderen Bäume begrüßten sie mit einem Lied, ihre Stimmen voller Dankbarkeit.

„Danke, Tilly", sagte Oakley. „Du hast uns gerettet."

Tilly lächelte und setzte sich unter die breiten Äste von Oakley, fühlte die Wärme der Sonne und das sanfte Rauschen der Blätter um sich herum. „Ich habe es nicht allein getan", sagte sie. „Wir haben es zusammen geschafft."

Von diesem Tag an besuchte Tilly die sprechenden Bäume oft, wo sie sangen, tanzten und Geschichten erzählten. Der Wald blieb ein magischer Ort, geschützt und geschätzt, dank eines mutigen kleinen Mädchens und der Kraft des Reims.

The Enormous Elephant Surprise

Once upon a time, in the fanciest mansion on the richest street of the wealthiest city, lived a girl named Penelope Plumwood. Penelope was not just any girl—she was fabulously, outrageously spoiled. Her bedroom was so big it had its own swimming pool, her wardrobe so vast that she could wear a different outfit every day of the year, and her toy collection could fill a department store. But no matter how much she had, Penelope always wanted more.

As her eleventh birthday approached, Penelope became fixated on getting the most extravagant gift possible. "I want something no one else has!" she declared, her diamond-studded shoes clicking on the marble floors as she stormed into the grand dining room where her parents were having tea.

Her father, who always wore a suit that cost more than a car, glanced at her from behind his newspaper. "What about a new yacht, darling?"

"Or perhaps a personal jet?" her mother added, stirring her tea with a silver spoon.

Penelope crossed her arms and pouted. "Boring. I want something BIG. Something alive. Something... magnificent!"

Her parents exchanged a glance, and after a moment, her father smiled. "How about an elephant?"

Penelope's eyes widened with excitement. An elephant! Now that would be a present to impress everyone at school. No one else had an elephant.

"Yes! I want an elephant for my birthday!" she shrieked, jumping up and down.

True to their word, her parents made the necessary arrangements. On the morning of her eleventh birthday, Penelope rushed down the sweeping staircase to find a very large, very wrinkly, very real elephant standing in the middle of their perfectly manicured lawn. A large, pink bow sat awkwardly atop its head, and it was surrounded by Penelope's family, friends, and a team of confused zookeepers.

"Surprise!" her parents beamed, while Penelope's classmates gasped in awe.

Penelope squealed with delight. "I shall name her Princess Petunia!" she declared, already imagining the envy on her friends' faces.

But as the days went by, Penelope quickly learned that having an elephant was not as glamorous as she had thought.

First of all, Princess Petunia was enormous. She couldn't fit inside the mansion, which Penelope thought was quite rude of the elephant. So, she had to stay in the garden, which soon turned into a muddy mess from all of Petunia's stomping.

Then, there was the food. Petunia ate a lot. Every day, truckloads of hay, fruits, and vegetables were delivered, and Penelope was expected to feed her. "I have to do it myself?" Penelope whined, but her parents insisted.

On top of that, elephants needed to bathe, and Penelope learned this the hard way when Petunia used the mansion's fountain as her personal bath. Water sprayed everywhere, soaking Penelope and her pristine clothes.

"This is a disaster!" Penelope cried, staring at the soggy remains of her designer outfit. "I didn't ask for a messy elephant!"

But the worst part was the smell. No amount of perfume could cover the... ahem... natural scent of an elephant.

Penelope tried to hide her growing frustration, but it was hard. The other girls at school, who had been jealous at first, now laughed at her behind her back. "How's your pet elephant, Penelope?" they teased. "Bet your house smells like a zoo!"

Penelope's pride was wounded, but she was too stubborn to admit she couldn't handle it.

One afternoon, after a particularly exhausting day of trying to clean up after Petunia's muddy escapades, Penelope stormed into the garden. "You're the worst birthday present ever!" she yelled, tears of frustration rolling down her cheeks.

Princess Petunia, who had been calmly munching on some leaves, turned her big, kind eyes toward Penelope. She raised her trunk and gently patted Penelope on the head, as if to say, I'm sorry.

Penelope blinked. She hadn't expected such a tender response from her giant pet. Slowly, she realized that maybe it wasn't Petunia's fault. After all, Petunia was just being an elephant.

Feeling a pang of guilt, Penelope sat down on the grass next to her. "It's not your fault, is it, Petunia?" she sighed. "I didn't think about what it would be like to take care of you. I just wanted something big and impressive."

Petunia nuzzled her trunk against Penelope's cheek, making her giggle despite herself. For the first time, Penelope really looked at her elephant—her big, loyal friend who hadn't asked to live in a mansion or be covered in pink bows.

"I haven't been fair to you, have I?" Penelope whispered, stroking Petunia's rough skin. "I've been so busy thinking about how you could make me look good, I forgot to take care of you properly."

From that moment on, Penelope's attitude began to change. She asked the zookeepers to help her understand how to take care of an elephant. She learned how to feed Petunia the right diet, how to bathe her properly, and even how to give her the exercise she needed.

Taking care of Petunia was still hard work, but Penelope found that the more effort she put into it, the more she grew to love her enormous pet. Petunia, in return, became more affectionate, and the two of them formed a bond that was more valuable to Penelope than impressing anyone at school.

As time passed, Penelope began to understand something even more important. She had been given many things in her life—fancy toys, expensive clothes, and extravagant gifts—but none of them had taught her responsibility or compassion. Petunia, however, had.

One sunny afternoon, Penelope's parents watched from the terrace as their daughter played happily in the garden with her elephant, both of them splashing around in a large pool Penelope had specially built for Petunia.

"I think our Penelope has changed," her mother said with a smile.

Her father nodded. "It seems the elephant was a good idea after all."

And they were right. Penelope had changed. She was no longer the spoiled, selfish girl who only thought about herself. Thanks to Princess Petunia, Penelope had learned the importance of responsibility, empathy, and taking care of others.

Now, when people asked Penelope what she got for her eleventh birthday, she didn't say, "An elephant." Instead, she smiled and replied, "A best friend."

Die Enorme Elefantenüberraschung

E s war einmal in der prächtigsten Villa der reichsten Straße der wohlhabendsten Stadt, ein Mädchen namens Penelope Plumwood. Penelope war nicht einfach nur ein Mädchen – sie war fabulös und extrem verwöhnt. Ihr Schlafzimmer war so groß, dass es einen eigenen Swimmingpool hatte, ihr Kleiderschrank war so riesig, dass sie an jedem Tag des Jahres ein anderes Outfit tragen konnte, und ihre Spielzeugsammlung hätte ein Kaufhaus füllen können. Aber egal, wie viel sie hatte, Penelope wollte immer mehr.

Als ihr elfter Geburtstag näher rückte, fixierte sich Penelope darauf, das extravaganteste Geschenk zu bekommen, das möglich war. „Ich will etwas, das sonst niemand hat!" erklärte sie, während ihre mit Diamanten besetzten Schuhe auf den Marmorböden klickten, als sie in das große Esszimmer stürmte, wo ihre Eltern Tee tranken.

Ihr Vater, der immer einen Anzug trug, der mehr kostete als ein Auto, blickte über die Zeitung hinweg zu ihr. „Wie wäre es mit einer neuen Yacht, Liebling?"

„Oder vielleicht einem Privatjet?" fügte ihre Mutter hinzu und rührte mit einem silbernen Löffel in ihrem Tee.

Penelope verschränkte die Arme und schmollte. „Langweilig. Ich will etwas GROßES. Etwas Lebendiges. Etwas... Großartiges!"

Ihre Eltern tauschten einen Blick aus, und nach einem Moment lächelte ihr Vater. „Wie wäre es mit einem Elefanten?"

Penelopes Augen weiteten sich vor Aufregung. Ein Elefant! Das wäre ein Geschenk, um alle in der Schule zu beeindrucken. Niemand sonst hatte einen Elefanten.

„Ja! Ich will einen Elefanten zu meinem Geburtstag!" kreischte sie und hüpfte aufgeregt auf und ab.

Wie versprochen, organisierten ihre Eltern alles Notwendige. Am Morgen ihres elften Geburtstags rannte Penelope die große Treppe hinunter und fand einen sehr großen, sehr faltigen, sehr echten Elefanten, der mitten auf ihrem perfekt gepflegten Rasen stand. Eine große, pinke Schleife saß unbeholfen auf seinem Kopf, und er war umgeben von Penelopes Familie, Freunden und einem Team verwirrter Tierpfleger.

„Überraschung!" strahlten ihre Eltern, während Penelopes Klassenkameraden in Ehrfurcht keuchten.

Penelope quietschte vor Freude. „Ich nenne sie Prinzessin Petunia!" verkündete sie und stellte sich bereits den Neid auf den Gesichtern ihrer Freunde vor.

Doch je mehr Tage vergingen, desto schneller lernte Penelope, dass es nicht so glamourös war, einen Elefanten zu haben, wie sie gedacht hatte.

Zuerst einmal war Prinzessin Petunia enorm. Sie konnte nicht ins Herrenhaus passen, was Penelope für ziemlich unhöflich von dem Elefanten hielt. Also musste sie im Garten bleiben, der bald wegen Petunias Tritten in ein schlammiges Chaos verwandelt wurde.

Dann war da das Futter. Petunia aß eine Menge. Jeden Tag wurden Lkw-Ladungen mit Heu, Obst und Gemüse geliefert, und Penelope wurde aufgefordert, sie zu füttern. „Muss ich das selbst machen?" jammerte Penelope, aber ihre Eltern bestanden darauf.

Außerdem benötigten Elefanten ein Bad, und Penelope lernte dies auf die harte Tour, als Petunia den Brunnen des Herrenhauses als ihr persönliches Bad benutzte. Wasser spritzte überall hin und durchnässte Penelope und ihre makellosen Kleider.

„Das ist eine Katastrophe!" schrie Penelope und starrte auf die durchnässten Überreste ihres Designer-Outfits. „Ich habe nicht nach einem schmutzigen Elefanten gefragt!"

Aber der schlimmste Teil war der Geruch. Kein Parfüm konnte den... ähem... natürlichen Duft eines Elefanten überdecken.

Penelope versuchte, ihre wachsende Frustration zu verbergen, aber es war schwer. Die anderen Mädchen in der Schule, die zunächst neidisch gewesen waren, lachten jetzt hinter ihrem Rücken über sie. „Wie geht's deinem Haustier-Elefanten, Penelope?" hänselten sie. „Wette, dein Haus riecht wie ein Zoo!"

Penelopes Stolz war verletzt, aber sie war zu stur, um zuzugeben, dass sie es nicht bewältigen konnte.

Eines Nachmittags, nach einem besonders anstrengenden Tag, an dem sie versucht hatte, nach Petunias schlammigen

Eskapaden aufzuräumen, stürmte Penelope in den Garten. „Du bist das schlimmste Geburtstagsgeschenk aller Zeiten!" schrie sie, während Tränen der Frustration über ihre Wangen rollten.

Prinzessin Petunia, die friedlich an einigen Blättern knabberte, wandte ihre großen, freundlichen Augen Penelope zu. Sie hob ihren Rüssel und patschte sanft Penelope auf den Kopf, als wollte sie sagen: Es tut mir leid.

Penelope blinzelte. Sie hatte nicht mit einer so zärtlichen Reaktion von ihrem riesigen Haustier gerechnet. Langsam wurde ihr klar, dass es vielleicht nicht Petunias Schuld war. Immerhin war Petunia einfach nur ein Elefant.

Ein Schuldgefühl überkam Penelope, und sie setzte sich auf das Gras neben ihr. „Es ist nicht deine Schuld, oder, Petunia?" seufzte sie. „Ich habe nicht darüber nachgedacht, wie es wäre, mich um dich zu kümmern. Ich wollte einfach nur etwas Großes und Beeindruckendes."

Petunia stupste ihren Rüssel an Penelopes Wange, was sie trotz sich selbst zum Kichern brachte. Zum ersten Mal sah Penelope ihren Elefanten wirklich – ihre große, treue Freundin, die nicht darum gebeten hatte, in einem Herrenhaus zu leben oder mit pinken Schleifen geschmückt zu werden.

„Ich war nicht fair zu dir, oder?" flüsterte Penelope und streichelte Petunias raue Haut. „Ich war so beschäftigt damit, darüber nachzudenken, wie du mich gut aussehen lassen könntest, dass ich vergessen habe, mich richtig um dich zu kümmern."

Von diesem Moment an begann sich Penelopes Einstellung zu ändern. Sie bat die Tierpfleger um Hilfe, um zu verstehen, wie man sich um einen Elefanten kümmert. Sie lernte, wie man Petunia die richtige Nahrung gab, wie man sie richtig badete und sogar, wie man ihr die Bewegung gab, die sie brauchte.

Es war immer noch harte Arbeit, sich um Petunia zu kümmern, aber Penelope stellte fest, dass sie, je mehr Mühe sie investierte, desto mehr sie ihre riesige Haustierfreundin liebte. Petunia hingegen wurde liebevoller, und die beiden bildeten eine Verbindung, die für Penelope wertvoller war als die Bewunderung anderer in der Schule.

Mit der Zeit begann Penelope zu verstehen, dass sie etwas noch Wichtigeres gelernt hatte. Sie hatte in ihrem Leben viele Dinge bekommen – schicke Spielzeuge, teure Kleidung und extravagante Geschenke –, aber keines von ihnen hatte ihr Verantwortung oder Mitgefühl beigebracht. Petunia jedoch hatte es getan.

An einem sonnigen Nachmittag beobachteten Penelopes Eltern von der Terrasse aus, wie ihre Tochter glücklich im Garten mit ihrem Elefanten spielte, während beide in einem großen Pool planschten, den Penelope speziell für Petunia gebaut hatte.

„Ich glaube, unsere Penelope hat sich verändert," sagte ihre Mutter mit einem Lächeln.

Ihr Vater nickte. „Es scheint, als war der Elefant doch eine gute Idee."

Und sie hatten recht. Penelope hatte sich verändert. Sie war nicht mehr das verwöhnte, egoistische Mädchen, das nur an sich selbst dachte. Dank Prinzessin Petunia hatte Penelope die Bedeutung von Verantwortung, Empathie und der Pflege anderer gelernt.

Jetzt, wenn die Leute Penelope fragten, was sie zu ihrem elften Geburtstag bekommen hatte, sagte sie nicht: „Einen Elefanten." Stattdessen lächelte sie und antwortete: „Eine beste Freundin."

Mr. Bumble's Strange Invention

In a small, quirky village, not far from the woods where strange things sometimes happened, lived an eccentric inventor by the name of Mr. Bumble. Mr. Bumble was known for his outlandish creations, ranging from clocks that could sing to chairs that could dance. However, his latest invention would soon become the most talked-about in the entire town—for better or for worse.

Mr. Bumble lived in a tall, crooked house at the end of Curly Lane, surrounded by a garden full of peculiar, colorful contraptions. One day, he burst out of his house, wearing his usual mismatched socks and an oversized coat full of tools, waving his arms and shouting, "I've done it! I've created the greatest invention of all time!"

The villagers, used to his antics, barely looked up from their tasks. But one person did—a curious young girl named Penny, who loved inventing things herself. She was always tinkering with gadgets in her parents' garage, so Mr. Bumble's wild declarations piqued her interest.

"What have you invented this time, Mr. Bumble?" Penny called out as she approached his house.

"Oh, Penny, my dear girl!" Mr. Bumble exclaimed, his eyes wide with excitement behind his thick, round glasses. "It's a machine like no other! It can turn anything into candy! Books, clothes, furniture—anything!"

Penny's eyes widened. "Anything into candy? That sounds... amazing! But also a little dangerous."

"Nonsense!" Mr. Bumble waved a dismissive hand. "Think of the possibilities! A world where anything you touch can become a delicious treat! No more boring meals, no more tasteless furniture. Why, you could turn your breakfast plate into a candy pancake, your shoes into marshmallow boots, even your—"

"Mr. Bumble," Penny interrupted, "have you tested it?"

Mr. Bumble looked slightly offended. "Of course I have! Well... sort of."

Penny raised an eyebrow. "Sort of?"

"Well, I've tested it on a few small things," Mr. Bumble admitted. "Like this!" He reached into his pocket and pulled out a shiny, red apple. He placed it on the ground, and from under his coat, he pulled out a strange-looking device. It had gears, pipes, and buttons all over it, and at the top was a large, funnel-like attachment.

"This," Mr. Bumble said proudly, "is my Candy Converter 3000."

He aimed the funnel at the apple and pressed a large green button. The machine hummed and whirred, spitting out puffs of steam and shooting out sparks. With a sudden "POP," the apple transformed into a perfectly wrapped candy apple, complete with a shiny red wrapper.

Penny gasped. "That's amazing! But, Mr. Bumble, what if the machine turns the wrong things into candy?"

"Nonsense!" Mr. Bumble said again, looking far too pleased with himself. "I have it under control."

But as Penny stared at the Candy Converter 3000, she couldn't shake a strange feeling that things were about to go terribly wrong.

Over the next few days, word spread about Mr. Bumble's invention. People from all over the village came to his house, begging him to turn their belongings into candy. Soon, there were candy chairs, candy teacups, and even candy hats. Everyone was thrilled with the new sugary world they were living in.

Except Penny.

While everyone else was turning their homes into candy palaces, Penny noticed something odd. The machine wasn't just transforming objects people wanted into candy—it was starting to act on its own.

One afternoon, as Penny walked through the village, she spotted Mrs. Fizzlewood, the town librarian, in front of the library. "Hello, Penny dear," Mrs. Fizzlewood said, "I'm just out for a stroll. Isn't this candy craze delightful?"

But as they talked, Penny's eyes widened in horror. The entire library behind Mrs. Fizzlewood was slowly being transformed into a gigantic chocolate building, with gumdrop doorknobs and caramel-covered bookshelves. Books were turning into licorice strips, their words vanishing as they melted into sticky goo.

Penny rushed to the library door, but it was too late. The last shelf of books turned into peppermint sticks before her eyes.

"This isn't good," Penny muttered to herself. "If the machine keeps going like this, it'll turn everything in town into candy—including people!"

Her fears were confirmed when, later that day, she saw Mr. Bumble himself standing in front of his house, desperately trying to stop the Candy Converter 3000, which had gone completely haywire. It was zapping everything in sight—trees, street lamps, even a passing bicycle—into various sweets.

"Oh no, oh no, oh no!" Mr. Bumble wailed, running around in circles as his hat turned into a giant marshmallow.

"Mr. Bumble!" Penny shouted. "We have to stop the machine!"

"I know, I know!" Mr. Bumble replied, "but I can't figure out how!"

Penny took a deep breath. "We need to think. What if we reverse the machine's process? Maybe it can turn things back to normal."

Mr. Bumble's eyes lit up. "Brilliant idea! But how?"

Penny thought for a moment. "What's the opposite of candy? Something... plain, simple, and not sweet at all!"

"Vegetables!" Mr. Bumble exclaimed.

Penny grinned. "Exactly! We'll need to reprogram the machine to turn things into vegetables. It's the only way to balance it out!"

Working quickly, Penny and Mr. Bumble began tweaking the machine. Penny adjusted the gears while Mr. Bumble frantically swapped the candy buttons for vegetable-themed ones. "Carrot button, lettuce lever... here we go!" Mr. Bumble muttered.

"Ready?" Penny asked, as she aimed the funnel at a candy streetlamp that was now made entirely of gummy bears.

Mr. Bumble nodded, his marshmallow hat wobbling on his head.

Penny pressed the new orange button, and the machine hummed loudly. It shot out a green beam, and with a loud PLOP, the gummy bear streetlamp transformed back into a regular one, but with a slight twist—it was now made of broccoli!

"It worked!" Penny cheered.

They ran through the village, zapping everything the machine had candified. A candy house turned into a sturdy pumpkin patch. A chocolate fountain became a celery stalk water feature. And the once-gumdrop library was restored, though it now had a few leafy vegetable books.

But just when they thought the chaos was over, they heard a voice behind them.

"Help! Help me!"

Penny and Mr. Bumble turned around to see... Mrs. Fizzlewood! She was standing, frozen in place, her entire body turned into a gigantic jellybean!

"Oh no!" Penny gasped. "We have to save her!"

Thinking quickly, she adjusted the machine one last time and aimed it at Mrs. Fizzlewood. "Hang in there!" she called, pressing the button.

In an instant, Mrs. Fizzlewood was back to her old self—though her hat was now a cabbage.

"Oh, my stars!" Mrs. Fizzlewood exclaimed, looking herself over. "I thought I was going to be a jellybean forever!"

Penny sighed in relief. "That was too close."

After that day, Mr. Bumble decided to put the Candy Converter 3000 away for good. The village returned to normal—well, mostly. Some things, like the broccoli streetlamp and vegetable furniture, remained, but the villagers didn't seem to mind.

As for Penny, she had proven herself to be the town's new inventor-in-chief. With her quick thinking and ingenuity, she had saved the day—and everyone knew it.

Mr. Bumble, while still as eccentric as ever, had learned an important lesson: just because you can turn everything into candy, doesn't mean you should.

And Penny? She continued to tinker and invent, but she always made sure to think through the consequences of her ideas. After all, the world didn't need any more jellybean librarians!

Mr. Bumbles seltsame Erfindung

In einem kleinen, skurrilen Dorf, nicht weit von den Wäldern, in denen manchmal merkwürdige Dinge geschahen, lebte ein exzentrischer Erfinder namens Mr. Bumble. Mr. Bumble war bekannt für seine außergewöhnlichen Kreationen, die von singenden Uhren bis zu tanzenden Stühlen reichten. Doch seine neueste Erfindung würde bald das meistdiskutierte Thema im ganzen Ort werden – zum Guten oder zum Schlechten.

Mr. Bumble wohnte in einem hohen, schiefen Haus am Ende der Lockenstraße, umgeben von einem Garten voller eigenartiger, bunter Apparate. Eines Tages stürmte er aus seinem Haus, trug seine üblichen unpassenden Socken und einen übergroßen Mantel voller Werkzeuge, schwenkte die Arme und rief: „Ich habe es geschafft! Ich habe die größte Erfindung aller Zeiten geschaffen!"

Die Dorfbewohner, die an seine Eskapaden gewöhnt waren, blickten kaum von ihren Aufgaben auf. Aber eine Person tat es – ein neugieriges kleines Mädchen namens Penny, das selbst gerne Dinge erfand. Sie bastelte ständig an Geräten in der Garage ihrer Eltern, also weckten Mr. Bumbles wildert Erklärungen ihr Interesse.

„Was hast du diesmal erfunden, Mr. Bumble?" rief Penny, als sie sich seinem Haus näherte.

„Oh, Penny, mein liebes Mädchen!" rief Mr. Bumble aus, seine Augen hinter seinen dicken, runden Brillen weit aufgerissen vor Aufregung. „Es ist eine Maschine wie keine andere! Sie kann alles in Süßigkeiten verwandeln! Bücher, Kleidung, Möbel – alles!"

Pennys Augen wurden groß. „Alles in Süßigkeiten? Das klingt... erstaunlich! Aber auch ein bisschen gefährlich."

„Unsinn!" Mr. Bumble wischte mit der Hand abweisend. „Denk an die Möglichkeiten! Eine Welt, in der alles, was du berührst, zu einer köstlichen Leckerei werden kann! Keine langweiligen Mahlzeiten mehr, keine geschmacklosen Möbel. Warum, du könntest deinen Frühstücksteller in einen süßen Pfannkuchen verwandeln, deine Schuhe in Schaumstoffstiefel, sogar deine –"

„Mr. Bumble," unterbrach Penny, „hast du es getestet?"

Mr. Bumble sah leicht beleidigt aus. „Natürlich habe ich das! Nun... irgendwie."

Penny hob eine Augenbraue. „Irgendwie?"

„Nun, ich habe es an ein paar kleinen Dingen getestet," gestand Mr. Bumble. „Wie diesem hier!" Er griff in seine Tasche und zog einen glänzenden, roten Apfel heraus. Er stellte ihn auf den Boden und zog ein seltsam aussehendes Gerät unter seinem Mantel hervor. Es hatte Zahnräder, Rohre und Knöpfe überall, und oben war ein großer, trichterförmiger Anhang.

„Das hier," sagte Mr. Bumble stolz, „ist mein Candy Converter 3000."

Er zielte mit dem Trichter auf den Apfel und drückte einen großen grünen Knopf. Die Maschine summte und surrte, stieß Dampfwölkchen aus und schoss Funken. Mit einem plötzlichen „PLOPP" verwandelte sich der Apfel in einen perfekt verpackten Zuckerapfel, komplett mit einer glänzenden roten Verpackung.

Penny schnappte nach Luft. „Das ist erstaunlich! Aber, Mr. Bumble, was ist, wenn die Maschine die falschen Dinge in Süßigkeiten verwandelt?"

„Unsinn!" sagte Mr. Bumble erneut, viel zu zufrieden mit sich selbst. „Ich habe das unter Kontrolle."

Doch während Penny auf den Candy Converter 3000 starrte, konnte sie ein seltsames Gefühl nicht abschütteln, dass etwas schrecklich schiefgehen würde.

In den nächsten Tagen verbreitete sich das Gerücht über Mr. Bumbles Erfindung. Menschen aus dem ganzen Dorf kamen zu seinem Haus und baten ihn, ihre Besitztümer in Süßigkeiten zu verwandeln. Bald gab es Zuckerstühle, Zuckertassen und sogar Zuckermützen. Alle waren begeistert von der neuen zuckerhaltigen Welt, in der sie lebten.

Außer Penny.

Während alle anderen ihre Häuser in Süßigkeitenpaläste verwandelten, bemerkte Penny etwas Merkwürdiges. Die Maschine verwandelte nicht nur die Objekte, die die Menschen wollten, in Süßigkeiten – sie begann, eigenständig zu agieren.

An einem Nachmittag, als Penny durch das Dorf spazierte, sah sie Mrs. Fizzlewood, die Bibliothekarin des Dorfes, vor der Bibliothek stehen. „Hallo, Penny, mein Schatz," sagte Mrs. Fizzlewood, „ich bin nur auf einem Spaziergang. Ist dieser Süßigkeiten-Wahnsinn nicht entzückend?"

Aber während sie sprachen, weiteten sich Pennys Augen vor Entsetzen. Die ganze Bibliothek hinter Mrs. Fizzlewood verwandelte sich langsam in ein riesiges Schokoladengebäude, mit Gummibärchen-Türknäufen und karamelüberzogenen Bücherregalen. Bücher verwandelten sich in Lakritzstreifen, deren Worte verschwanden, während sie in klebrigen Brei schmolzen.

Penny rannte zur Bibliothekstür, aber es war zu spät. Das letzte Regal mit Büchern verwandelte sich vor ihren Augen in Pfefferminzstäbchen.

„Das ist nicht gut," murmelte Penny vor sich hin. „Wenn die Maschine so weitermacht, verwandelt sie alles im Dorf in Süßigkeiten – einschließlich der Menschen!"

Ihre Ängste wurden bestätigt, als sie später am Tag Mr. Bumble selbst vor seinem Haus stehen sah, der verzweifelt versuchte, den Candy Converter 3000 zu stoppen, der völlig verrückt gespielt hatte. Er zapfte alles in Sichtweite an – Bäume, Straßenlaternen, sogar ein vorbeifahrendes Fahrrad – in verschiedene Süßigkeiten.

„Oh nein, oh nein, oh nein!" jammerte Mr. Bumble, während er im Kreis lief und sein Hut sich in einen riesigen Marshmallow verwandelte.

„Mr. Bumble!" rief Penny. „Wir müssen die Maschine stoppen!"

„Ich weiß, ich weiß!" antwortete Mr. Bumble, „aber ich kann nicht herausfinden, wie!"

Penny atmete tief ein. „Wir müssen nachdenken. Was wäre, wenn wir den Prozess der Maschine umkehren? Vielleicht kann sie die Dinge wieder normal machen."

Mr. Bumbles Augen leuchteten auf. „Brillante Idee! Aber wie?"

Penny dachte einen Moment nach. „Was ist das Gegenteil von Süßigkeiten? Etwas... schlicht, einfach und gar nicht süß!"

„Gemüse!" rief Mr. Bumble.

Penny grinste. „Genau! Wir müssen die Maschine umprogrammieren, damit sie die Dinge in Gemüse verwandelt. Das ist der einzige Weg, um das Gleichgewicht wiederherzustellen!"

Schnell arbeiteten Penny und Mr. Bumble daran, die Maschine zu modifizieren. Penny stellte die Zahnräder ein, während Mr. Bumble hektisch die Süßigkeitentasten gegen Gemüse-Themen-Tasten austauschte. „Karottenknopf, Salathebel... los geht's!" murmelte Mr. Bumble.

„Bereit?" fragte Penny, als sie den Trichter auf eine Zuckerlaterne zielte, die jetzt ganz aus Gummibärchen bestand.

Mr. Bumble nickte, sein Marshmallowhut wackelte auf seinem Kopf.

Penny drückte den neuen orangenen Knopf, und die Maschine summte laut. Sie schoss einen grünen Strahl aus, und mit einem lauten PLUMS verwandelte sich die Gummibärchenlaterne zurück in eine normale, aber mit einer kleinen Wendung – sie war jetzt aus Brokkoli!

„Es hat funktioniert!" jubelte Penny.

Sie rannten durch das Dorf und zapften alles an, was die Maschine in Süßigkeiten verwandelt hatte. Ein Zuckerhaus verwandelte sich in ein robustes Kürbisfeld. Ein Schokoladenbrunnen wurde zu einem Selleriestock-Wassermerkmal. Und die einstige Gummibärchenbibliothek wurde wiederhergestellt, obwohl sie jetzt ein paar blättrige Gemüse-Bücher hatte.

Aber gerade als sie dachten, das Chaos sei vorbei, hörten sie eine Stimme hinter sich.

„Hilfe! Helft mir!"

Penny und Mr. Bumble drehten sich um und sahen... Mrs. Fizzlewood! Sie stand bewegungslos da, ihr ganzer Körper war in einen riesigen Gummibär verwandelt worden!

„Oh nein!" schnappte Penny. „Wir müssen sie retten!"

Schnell dachte sie nach, stellte die Maschine ein letztes Mal ein und zielte auf Mrs. Fizzlewood. „Halte durch!" rief sie und drückte den Knopf.

Im Nu war Mrs. Fizzlewood wieder sie selbst – obwohl ihr Hut jetzt ein Kohl war.

„Oh, meine Sterne!" rief Mrs. Fizzlewood und sah sich um. „Ich dachte, ich würde für immer ein Gummibär sein!"

Penny seufzte erleichtert. „Das war zu knapp."

Nach diesem Tag beschloss Mr. Bumble, den Candy Converter 3000 für immer wegzulegen. Das Dorf kehrte zur Normalität zurück—na ja, größtenteils. Einige Dinge, wie die Brokkoli-Straßenlaterne und die Gemüse-Möbel, blieben, aber die Dorfbewohner schienen sich nicht darum zu kümmern.

Was Penny angeht, so hatte sie sich als die neue Erfinderin des Dorfes bewiesen. Mit ihrem schnellen Denken und ihrer Einfallsreichtum hatte sie den Tag gerettet—und jeder wusste es.

Mr. Bumble hatte, obwohl er weiterhin so exzentrisch wie eh und je war, eine wichtige Lektion gelernt: Nur weil man alles in Süßigkeiten verwandeln kann, bedeutet das nicht, dass man es sollte.

Und Penny? Sie bastelte und erfand weiterhin, aber sie sorgte immer dafür, die Konsequenzen ihrer Ideen zu durchdenken. Schließlich brauchte die Welt keine weiteren Geleebohnen-Bibliothekare!

The Misbehaving Magic Paintbrush

Oliver was a boy with a wild imagination. In school, he would doodle in his notebooks instead of listening to the teacher. At home, he would sketch monsters, robots, and rockets, dreaming of them coming to life. He wasn't a bad boy—just mischievous. He loved pranks, especially ones that caused no real harm but left everyone laughing (well, except for the teachers and his parents).

One day, Oliver stumbled upon something that would change everything. He was walking home from school when he spotted a small, dusty shop tucked away at the end of an alley he had never noticed before. Its sign read, Madame Mirabel's Mystical Curiosities. The name alone was enough to draw him in.

Inside, the shop was cluttered with all sorts of strange and magical items—sparkling jars, glowing stones, and peculiar trinkets. But one thing, in particular, caught his eye: an old paintbrush, resting on a velvet cushion.

"That's the one," Madame Mirabel said, appearing out of nowhere behind him. She was a small, mysterious woman with eyes that seemed to know too much. "The paintbrush of infinite possibility."

Oliver, fascinated, asked, "What's so special about it?"

Madame Mirabel smiled a sly smile. "Anything you paint with it will come to life."

Oliver's heart skipped a beat. Anything? He had to have it. Without thinking twice, he traded his pocket money for the paintbrush and ran all the way home.

At home, Oliver wasted no time. He grabbed his sketchpad and began to draw. First, he painted a dog—an adorable little mutt with floppy ears and a wagging tail. As soon as he finished the last stroke, the paint shimmered, and the dog jumped off the page!

"Woof!" it barked, prancing around Oliver's room.

Oliver's jaw dropped. It worked! The dog was alive, just like Madame Mirabel had said. He spent hours playing fetch with it, laughing as the dog chased a bouncing ball around his room. But soon, Oliver's mischievous mind began to churn. What else could he paint?

Next, he painted a bicycle—only this one could fly. As he finished the drawing, the bike wobbled off the page and hovered in the air. Oliver hopped on, flying around his room in glee. The feeling of soaring just a few feet off the ground was exhilarating.

"Imagine the pranks I could pull with this!" he chuckled.

But what started as innocent fun quickly spiraled out of control.

Oliver's first prank was harmless enough. He painted a frog that could sing opera. It hopped through town, croaking out dramatic arias that confused and amused everyone. His classmates found it hilarious. Even his teachers couldn't help but laugh—at least for the first day.

But as the days passed, Oliver's pranks grew more elaborate. He painted a massive octopus, which slipped and slid through the school hallways, grabbing people's backpacks and juggling them in its many tentacles. He drew a giant bouncing ball that ricocheted off buildings, sending bicycles and trash cans flying in all directions.

The townspeople were less amused. Mr. Jenkins, the stern shopkeeper, had his store flooded with jellybeans after Oliver drew a candy machine gone wild. Mrs. Hopps, the head teacher, nearly fainted when a giant talking spider appeared on her desk during a lesson.

Oliver laughed and laughed. He loved the chaos. But he didn't realize that with each prank, the creations were becoming harder to control. They weren't just doing what Oliver had drawn them to do—they were starting to develop minds of their own.

One day, Oliver decided to pull his biggest prank yet. He painted a massive dragon, its scales glittering in every shade of the rainbow. This would be the ultimate prank, he thought. But as soon as the dragon crawled off the page, something was different. It didn't wait for instructions. It didn't follow Oliver's commands. Instead, it let out a deafening roar and flew straight out of Oliver's window.

Oliver's stomach dropped. He scrambled to catch the paintbrush, but it was too late. The dragon soared above the town, its enormous wings blocking out the sun. It swooped down and set the candy machine rolling again, creating a flood of sticky sweets that filled the streets. It knocked over lampposts with its tail and sent people running in all directions.

Even worse, Oliver's other creations started to act up. The octopus returned, grabbing anything it could find and tossing it in the air. The flying bike zoomed through the sky, nearly crashing into rooftops. The singing frog, now three times its original size, bellowed so loudly that windows rattled.

The town was in chaos, and it was all Oliver's fault.

As the town descended into madness, Oliver realized he had to fix his mistakes. He raced to find Madame Mirabel, hoping she would know what to do. When he finally reached her shop, he burst through the door, panting.

"Help!" he cried. "My drawings—they're out of control!"

Madame Mirabel didn't look surprised. She simply raised an eyebrow. "I warned you, didn't I? A paintbrush that brings things to life is not to be used lightly."

"I know," Oliver said, ashamed. "But how do I stop it?"

Madame Mirabel handed him a small bottle of glittering ink. "This is the Ink of Undoing. Paint over your creations, and they will return to the page. But be warned—this only works if you truly mean it. You must take responsibility for what you've done."

Oliver nodded, grabbing the bottle and running back to the town. As he approached the chaos, he took a deep breath. He would have to be brave.

First, he found the dragon, which was circling the town square, roaring at anyone who came near. Oliver dipped the paintbrush into the Ink of Undoing and carefully painted over the dragon's tail. As the brush touched the scales, the dragon began to shrink, its roars fading into nothing. Soon, it was nothing more than a colorful sketch on his sketchpad.

One by one, Oliver tracked down his misbehaving creations—the octopus, the flying bike, the oversized frog—and painted them back into the pages. It was hard work, and Oliver felt a pang of guilt with each stroke, realizing how much trouble he had caused.

When the last creation was safely back in the sketchpad, the town returned to normal—though it took a lot of scrubbing to get the jellybeans off the streets. The townspeople, at first furious, began to forgive Oliver when they saw how hard he worked to make things right.

From that day on, Oliver used the paintbrush much more carefully. He still drew fantastical things—talking animals and flying contraptions—but he made sure they were helpful, not harmful. And he learned that creativity, while powerful, came with great responsibility.

As for Madame Mirabel, she watched from afar, pleased that Oliver had learned his lesson. And the magical paintbrush? It remained with Oliver, but he always remembered to use it wisely.

Because in the end, Oliver realized that the greatest power wasn't in creating chaos, but in using his imagination for good.

Der Ungezogene Magische Pinsel

Oliver war ein Junge mit einer wilden Fantasie. In der Schule kritzelte er in seinen Notizheften, anstatt dem Lehrer zuzuhören. Zu Hause skizzierte er Monster, Roboter und Raketen und träumte davon, dass sie zum Leben erwachen würden. Er war kein böser Junge – nur schelmisch. Er liebte Streiche, besonders solche, die keinen echten Schaden anrichteten, aber alle zum Lachen brachten (naja, außer den Lehrern und seinen Eltern).

Eines Tages stieß Oliver auf etwas, das alles verändern sollte. Er ging von der Schule nach Hause, als er ein kleines, staubiges Geschäft entdeckte, das am Ende einer Gasse lag, die ihm zuvor nie aufgefallen war. Das Schild darüber lautete: Madame Mirabels Mystische Kuriositäten. Der Name allein reichte aus, um ihn anzuziehen.

Drinnen war der Laden vollgestopft mit allerlei seltsamen und magischen Gegenständen – funkelnden Gläsern, leuchtenden Steinen und merkwürdigen Andenken. Aber eines fiel ihm besonders ins Auge: ein alter Pinsel, der auf einem Samtkissen lag.

„Das ist der Richtige", sagte Madame Mirabel und erschien wie aus dem Nichts hinter ihm. Sie war eine kleine, geheimnisvolle Frau mit Augen, die schienen, als wüssten sie zu viel. „Der Pinsel der unendlichen Möglichkeiten."

Oliver, fasziniert, fragte: „Was ist so besonders daran?"

Madame Mirabel lächelte verschmitzt. „Alles, was du damit malst, wird lebendig."

Olivers Herz machte einen Satz. Alles? Er musste ihn haben. Ohne zweimal nachzudenken, tauschte er sein Taschengeld gegen den Pinsel und rannte den ganzen Weg nach Hause.

Zu Hause ließ Oliver keine Zeit verstreichen. Er schnappte sich seinen Skizzenblock und begann zu zeichnen. Zuerst malte er einen Hund – einen niedlichen kleinen Mischling mit schlappenden Ohren und einem wedelnden Schwanz. Kaum hatte er den letzten Strich vollendet, funkelte die Farbe, und der Hund sprang von der Seite!

„Wuff!" bellte er und hüpfte fröhlich durch Olivers Zimmer.

Olivers Kinnlade klappte herunter. Es funktionierte! Der Hund war lebendig, genau wie Madame Mirabel gesagt hatte. Stundenlang spielte er mit ihm Apportieren und lachte, während der Hund einem hüpfenden Ball hinterherjagte. Doch bald begann Olivers schelmischer Verstand zu arbeiten. Was konnte er noch malen?

Als Nächstes malte er ein Fahrrad – nur dieses konnte fliegen. Als er die Zeichnung beendete, wackelte das Rad von der Seite und schwebte in der Luft. Oliver schwang sich auf und flog fröhlich durch sein Zimmer. Das Gefühl, nur ein paar Fuß über dem Boden zu schweben, war berauschend.

„Stell dir die Streiche vor, die ich damit aushecken könnte!" kicherte er.

Doch was als harmloser Spaß begann, geriet schnell außer Kontrolle.

Olivers erster Streich war harmlos genug. Er malte einen Frosch, der Oper sang. Er hüpfte durch die Stadt und quakte dramatische Arien, die alle verwirrten und amüsierten. Seine Klassenkameraden fanden es urkomisch. Sogar seine Lehrer konnten nicht anders, als zu lachen – zumindest am ersten Tag.

Aber mit den Tagen wurden Olivers Streiche immer ausgefallener. Er malte einen riesigen Oktopus, der durch die Schulflure rutschte und die Rucksäcke der Schüler in seinen vielen Tentakeln jonglierte. Er zeichnete einen riesigen hüpfenden Ball, der von den Gebäuden abprallte und Fahrräder und Mülleimer in alle Richtungen schleuderte.

Die Stadtbewohner fanden das weniger amüsant. Herr Jenkins, der strenge Ladenbesitzer, hatte seinen Laden nach Olivers Zeichnung einer verrückten Süßigkeitenmaschine mit Gummibärchen überflutet. Frau Hopps, die Schulleiterin, wäre fast ohnmächtig geworden, als während einer Unterrichtsstunde eine riesige sprechende Spinne auf ihrem Tisch erschien.

Oliver lachte und lachte. Er liebte das Chaos. Aber er bemerkte nicht, dass seine Kreationen mit jedem Streich schwerer zu kontrollieren wurden. Sie taten nicht nur, was Oliver ihnen aufgetragen hatte – sie begannen, eigene Gedanken zu entwickeln.

Eines Tages beschloss Oliver, seinen größten Streich zu ziehen. Er malte einen riesigen Drachen, dessen Schuppen in allen Regenbogenfarben glitzerten. Das würde der ultimative Streich sein, dachte er. Doch als der Drache von der Seite krabbelte, war etwas anders. Er wartete nicht auf Anweisungen. Er folgte nicht Olivers Befehlen. Stattdessen ließ er ein ohrenbetäubendes Brüllen los und flog direkt aus Olivers Fenster.

Olivers Magen fiel in die Tiefe. Er versuchte, den Pinsel zu fangen, aber es war zu spät. Der Drache schwebte über der Stadt, seine riesigen Flügel verdunkelten die Sonne. Er stürzte hinunter und ließ die Süßigkeitenmaschine wieder laufen, wodurch eine Flut von klebrigen Süßigkeiten die Straßen füllte. Mit seinem Schwanz stieß er Laternen um und ließ die Leute in alle Richtungen davonrennen.

Noch schlimmer war, dass auch Olivers andere Kreationen anfingen, verrückt zu spielen. Der Oktopus kam zurück, schnappte sich alles, was er finden konnte, und warf es in die Luft. Das fliegende Fahrrad sauste durch den Himmel und wäre beinahe gegen die Dächer gekracht. Der singende Frosch, jetzt dreimal so groß wie ursprünglich, quakte so laut, dass die Fenster klirrten.

Die Stadt war im Chaos, und es war alles Olivers Schuld.

Als die Stadt ins Chaos versank, erkannte Oliver, dass er seine Fehler beheben musste. Er rannte, um Madame Mirabel zu finden, in der Hoffnung, dass sie wüsste, was zu tun war. Als er endlich ihr Geschäft erreichte, stürmte er durch die Tür und keuchte.

„Hilfe!" rief er. „Meine Zeichnungen – sie sind außer Kontrolle!"

Madame Mirabel sah nicht überrascht aus. Sie hob einfach eine Augenbraue. „Ich habe dich gewarnt, nicht wahr? Ein Pinsel, der Dinge zum Leben erweckt, sollte nicht leichtfertig verwendet werden."

„Ich weiß", sagte Oliver beschämt. „Aber wie stoppe ich es?"

Madame Mirabel reichte ihm eine kleine Flasche mit glitzernder Tinte. „Das ist die Tinte des Rückgängigmachens. Male über deine Kreationen, und sie kehren zurück auf die Seite. Aber sei gewarnt – das funktioniert nur, wenn du es wirklich ernst meinst. Du musst Verantwortung für das übernehmen, was du getan hast."

Oliver nickte, schnappte sich die Flasche und rannte zurück in die Stadt. Als er das Chaos sah, atmete er tief durch. Er musste mutig sein.

Zuerst fand er den Drachen, der über den Stadtplatz kreiste und jeden anbellte, der sich näherte. Oliver tauchte den Pinsel in die Tinte des Rückgängigmachens und malte vorsichtig über den Schwanz des Drachen. Als der Pinsel die Schuppen berührte, begann der Drache zu schrumpfen, sein Gebrüll verebbte. Bald war er nichts mehr als eine bunte Skizze in seinem Skizzenblock.

Eins nach dem anderen verfolgte Oliver seine ungezogenen Kreationen – den Oktopus, das fliegende Fahrrad, den übergroßen Frosch – und malte sie zurück auf die Seiten. Es war harte Arbeit, und Oliver verspürte bei jedem Strich ein schlechtes Gewissen, als ihm bewusst wurde, wie viel Unheil er angerichtet hatte.

Als die letzte Kreation sicher zurück im Skizzenblock war, kehrte die Stadt zur Normalität zurück – obwohl es viel Geschrubbe brauchte, um die Gummibärchen von den Straßen zu entfernen. Die Stadtbewohner, zunächst wütend, begannen Oliver zu vergeben, als sie sahen, wie hart er arbeitete, um alles in Ordnung zu bringen.

Von diesem Tag an verwendete Oliver den Pinsel viel sorgfältiger. Er zeichnete weiterhin fantastische Dinge – sprechende Tiere und fliegende Apparate – aber er sorgte dafür, dass sie hilfreich und nicht schädlich waren. Und er lernte, dass Kreativität, so mächtig sie auch war, mit großer Verantwortung einherging.

Was Madame Mirabel betrifft, so beobachtete sie aus der Ferne, erfreut darüber, dass Oliver seine Lektion gelernt hatte. Und der magische Pinsel? Er blieb bei Oliver, aber er erinnerte sich immer daran, ihn weise zu benutzen.

Denn am Ende erkannte Oliver, dass die größte Kraft nicht darin lag, Chaos zu schaffen, sondern seine Fantasie zum Guten zu nutzen.

The Flying Sweets of Whizzpop Lane

Whizzpop Lane was unlike any other street in the town of Muddlebrook. It was quiet, with neat little houses all lined up, but at the very end stood the most curious shop anyone had ever seen: Mrs. Figgle's Fanciful Confections. The sign above the door was covered in swirling colors, and every day, the sweet aroma of baking treats drifted down the lane, making everyone's mouths water.

Mrs. Figgle, the owner, was no ordinary baker. She was short and round, with twinkling eyes and always wore a hat that seemed to change shape depending on her mood. Some said she was a bit magical, and her sweets were known far and wide for being, well, extraordinary.

But even in a town full of peculiar things, no one could have expected the day when Mrs. Figgle invented her most magical treat yet.

It all began one summer afternoon. Mrs. Figgle was in her shop, humming to herself as she mixed a batch of sugar, syrup, and a mysterious ingredient she kept hidden in a jar labeled For Special Occasions Only.

"Now, this should do the trick!" she muttered, pouring the mixture into molds shaped like little clouds. As she pulled the tray from the oven, the sweets sparkled and gave off a faint, glowing mist.

"These," Mrs. Figgle said with a wink, "are going to be extra special."

When the sweets were ready, she placed them in the window with a new sign: Try Mrs. Figgle's Famous Flying Sweets! So Light, They'll Make You Float!

The children of Whizzpop Lane rushed to the shop the moment they saw the sign. Among them was Timmy, a boy with a big appetite and an even bigger sense of curiosity.

"One flying sweet, please!" Timmy said, handing over his pocket money.

Mrs. Figgle smiled warmly and handed him a small, glowing candy. "Just one," she said, "and remember—these sweets are magical. Eat too many, and who knows what might happen!"

Timmy nodded eagerly, barely listening. He popped the sweet into his mouth and felt a strange sensation. Suddenly, his feet lifted off the ground! He floated a few inches into the air, his arms waving in excitement.

"Look at me!" he shouted. "I'm flying!"

The other children watched in amazement as Timmy floated in the air for a few minutes before gently drifting back to the ground.

From that moment on, Mrs. Figgle's Flying Sweets became the talk of the town.

The next day, Timmy returned to the shop with his friends. They each bought a flying sweet and enjoyed floating around Whizzpop Lane for a few minutes before landing softly on the ground. It was all good fun.

But Timmy couldn't help but wonder—what would happen if he ate two flying sweets? Or three?

He waited until his friends had left, then sneaked back to Mrs. Figgle's shop.

"Two sweets today, Mrs. Figgle," he said, grinning.

Mrs. Figgle raised an eyebrow. "Are you sure, Timmy? I told you before—one sweet is enough to make you float. Any more, and you might get into trouble."

But Timmy was too excited to listen. He handed over his money and took the sweets, stuffing both into his mouth at once. The moment he swallowed, he felt himself lift off the ground—higher this time.

"Wow!" he shouted as he floated higher and higher above the shop. He could see the rooftops of Whizzpop Lane beneath him.

But then something strange happened. Timmy didn't stop floating. In fact, he was rising faster—much faster than before.

"Uh-oh," he muttered. "I think I've had too many!"

He tried waving his arms and kicking his legs, but it was no use. The more he struggled, the higher he floated. Soon, he was drifting over the trees and heading towards the clouds.

Down below, Timmy's friends saw what was happening.

"Timmy's floating away!" shouted Lucy, his best friend.

"We've got to do something!" cried Henry.

The children raced to Mrs. Figgle's shop, where they found the baker calmly stirring a pot of fudge.

"Mrs. Figgle! Timmy's floating too high!" Lucy gasped. "He ate too many flying sweets!"

Mrs. Figgle looked up, her eyes twinkling with amusement. "Oh dear, I did warn him, didn't I? But don't worry—we'll have him back down in no time."

She reached into a cupboard and pulled out a small, glowing jar. "This is Grounding Toffee," she explained. "One bite, and he'll come back down to earth like a feather."

"But how do we get it to him?" Henry asked, looking up at Timmy, who was now just a speck in the sky.

Mrs. Figgle smiled. "We'll need to work together. Lucy, you take this toffee and attach it to a balloon. Henry, you and I will fly up using our own sweets to guide the balloon to Timmy."

With Mrs. Figgle's instructions, Lucy tied the glowing toffee to a large balloon. Henry and Mrs. Figgle each popped a flying sweet into their mouths and gently floated into the air, guiding the balloon up towards Timmy.

Meanwhile, high above, Timmy was starting to panic. He could see nothing but clouds around him, and he was getting dizzy from the height.

"I'll never eat another sweet again!" he groaned. "Just get me down!"

At that moment, he saw something in the distance—a bright balloon floating towards him with Mrs. Figgle and Henry in tow.

"Grab the toffee!" Henry shouted as they got closer.

Timmy reached out, his hands trembling, and caught the toffee. He took a big bite, and instantly, he felt his body start to lower. Slowly, he floated back down to the ground, where his friends were waiting.

When his feet finally touched the earth, Timmy collapsed in relief.

"Thank you, thank you!" he said, looking around at his friends and Mrs. Figgle.

Mrs. Figgle patted Timmy on the shoulder. "Well, young man, I hope you've learned a valuable lesson today."

Timmy nodded, his face red with embarrassment. "I have! I promise I'll never eat too many sweets again."

"And remember," Mrs. Figgle said with a wink, "magic is best enjoyed in moderation."

The children all laughed, and Timmy, though a little shaken, joined in. From that day forward, Timmy stuck to just one flying sweet—just enough for a little fun, but never enough to send him soaring into the sky again.

As for Mrs. Figgle's magical sweets, they continued to be the talk of Whizzpop Lane, and the children of Muddlebrook enjoyed their gentle floating adventures—always remembering to follow the rules.

Because in the end, they all learned that too much of a good thing can send you a little too far off the ground!

Die fliegenden Süßigkeiten der Whizzpop Lane

Die Whizzpop Lane war unlike any other street in the Stadt Muddlebrook. Es war ruhig, mit hübschen kleinen Häusern, die alle aufgereiht waren, aber am Ende stand der merkwürdigste Laden, den man je gesehen hatte: Mrs. Figgles phantastische Süßigkeiten. Das Schild über der Tür war mit wirbelnden Farben bedeckt, und jeden Tag zog der süße Duft frisch gebackener Leckereien die Straße hinunter und ließ allen das Wasser im Munde zusammenlaufen.

Mrs. Figgle, die Besitzerin, war keine gewöhnliche Bäckerin. Sie war klein und rund, mit funkelnden Augen, und trug immer einen Hut, der je nach Stimmung seine Form zu ändern schien. Manche sagten, sie sei ein bisschen magisch, und ihre Süßigkeiten waren weit und breit dafür bekannt, nun ja, außergewöhnlich zu sein.

Aber selbst in einer Stadt voller seltsamer Dinge hätte niemand den Tag vorhersehen können, als Mrs. Figgle ihre bisher magischste Leckerei erfand.

Es begann alles an einem Sommernachmittag. Mrs. Figgle war in ihrem Laden und summte vor sich hin, während sie eine Mischung aus Zucker, Sirup und einer geheimnisvollen Zutat, die sie in einem Glas mit der Aufschrift Nur für besondere Anlässe versteckt hielt, zusammenrührte.

„Das sollte klappen!" murmelte sie und goss die Mischung in Formen, die wie kleine Wolken aussahen. Als sie das Blech aus dem Ofen zog, funkelten die Süßigkeiten und verströmten einen schwachen, leuchtenden Dunst.

„Diese," sagte Mrs. Figgle mit einem Augenzwinkern, „werden extra besonders."

Als die Süßigkeiten fertig waren, stellte sie sie ins Fenster mit einem neuen Schild: Probiert Mrs. Figgles berühmte fliegenden Süßigkeiten! So leicht, dass sie euch zum Schweben bringen!

Die Kinder der Whizzpop Lane rannten sofort zu dem Laden, als sie das Schild sahen. Unter ihnen war Timmy, ein Junge mit großem Appetit und noch größerer Neugier.

„Eine fliegende Süßigkeit, bitte!" sagte Timmy und gab sein Taschengeld.

Mrs. Figgle lächelte herzlich und reichte ihm eine kleine, leuchtende Süßigkeit. „Nur eine," sagte sie, „und denk daran—diese Süßigkeiten sind magisch. Iss zu viele, und wer weiß, was passieren könnte!"

Timmy nickte eifrig und hörte kaum zu. Er steckte die Süßigkeit in den Mund und fühlte ein seltsames Gefühl. Plötzlich hoben sich seine Füße vom Boden! Er schwebte ein paar Zentimeter in die Luft, seine Arme schwenkten vor Aufregung.

„Schaut mich an!" rief er. „Ich fliege!"

Die anderen Kinder schauten staunend zu, wie Timmy einige Minuten in der Luft schwebte, bevor er sanft zurück auf den Boden sank.

Von diesem Moment an wurden Mrs. Figgles fliegende Süßigkeiten zum Gesprächsthema der Stadt.

Am nächsten Tag kehrte Timmy mit seinen Freunden in den Laden zurück. Sie kauften sich alle eine fliegende Süßigkeit und hatten viel Spaß dabei, ein paar Minuten lang durch die Whizzpop Lane zu schweben, bevor sie sanft zu Boden landeten. Es war alles ein großer Spaß.

Aber Timmy konnte nicht anders, als sich zu fragen—was würde passieren, wenn er zwei fliegende Süßigkeiten aß? Oder drei?

Er wartete, bis seine Freunde gegangen waren, und schlich dann zurück zu Mrs. Figgles Laden.

„Zwei Süßigkeiten heute, Mrs. Figgle," sagte er und grinste.

Mrs. Figgle zog eine Augenbraue hoch. „Bist du dir sicher, Timmy? Ich habe dir schon vorher gesagt—eine Süßigkeit reicht aus, um dich zum Schweben zu bringen. Mehr, und du könntest in Schwierigkeiten geraten."

Aber Timmy war zu aufgeregt, um zuzuhören. Er gab sein Geld und nahm die Süßigkeiten, steckte beide gleichzeitig in den Mund. Im Moment, als er schluckte, fühlte er sich wieder vom Boden abheben—diesmal höher.

„Wow!" rief er, während er höher und höher über dem Laden schwebte. Er konnte die Dächer der Whizzpop Lane unter sich sehen.

Aber dann passierte etwas Seltsames. Timmy hörte nicht auf zu schweben. Tatsächlich stieg er schneller—viel schneller als zuvor.

„Uh-oh," murmelte er. „Ich glaube, ich habe zu viele gehabt!"

Er versuchte, seine Arme zu schwenken und seine Beine zu treten, aber es half nichts. Je mehr er sich anstrengte, desto höher schwebte er. Bald schwebte er über die Bäume und näherte sich den Wolken.

Unten sahen Timmys Freunde, was passierte.

„Timmy schwebt davon!" rief Lucy, seine beste Freundin.

„Wir müssen etwas unternehmen!" rief Henry.

Die Kinder rannten zu Mrs. Figgles Laden, wo sie die Bäckerin fanden, die gelassen einen Topf mit Fudge rührte.

„Mrs. Figgle! Timmy schwebt zu hoch!" keuchte Lucy. „Er hat zu viele fliegende Süßigkeiten gegessen!"

Mrs. Figgle sah auf und ihre Augen funkelten vor Vergnügen. „Oh je, ich habe ihn gewarnt, nicht wahr? Aber keine Sorge—wir bringen ihn in kürzester Zeit wieder herunter."

Sie griff in einen Schrank und zog ein kleines, leuchtendes Glas heraus. „Das ist Erdungs-Toffee," erklärte sie. „Ein Biss, und er wird wie eine Feder wieder auf den Boden zurückkommen."

„Aber wie bringen wir es zu ihm?" fragte Henry und schaute zu Timmy, der jetzt nur noch ein Punkt am Himmel war.

Mrs. Figgle lächelte. „Wir müssen zusammenarbeiten. Lucy, du nimmst dieses Toffee und befestigst es an einem Ballon. Henry, du und ich fliegen mit unseren eigenen Süßigkeiten, um den Ballon zu Timmy zu führen."

Nach Mrs. Figgles Anweisungen band Lucy das leuchtende Toffee an einen großen Ballon. Henry und Mrs. Figgle steckten sich jeder eine fliegende Süßigkeit in den Mund und schwebten sanft in die Luft, während sie den Ballon in Richtung Timmy führten.

Inzwischen begann Timmy hoch oben in Panik zu geraten. Er sah nichts als Wolken um sich und wurde schwindelig von der Höhe.

„Ich werde nie wieder eine Süßigkeit essen!" stöhnte er. „Holt mich einfach runter!"

In diesem Moment sah er in der Ferne etwas—einen hellen Ballon, der auf ihn zufloß, mit Mrs. Figgle und Henry im Schlepptau.

„Greif nach dem Toffee!" rief Henry, als sie näher kamen.

Timmy streckte die Hände aus, seine Hände zitterten, und griff nach dem Toffee. Er nahm einen großen Biss, und sofort spürte er, wie sein Körper zu sinken begann. Langsam schwebte er zurück zum Boden, wo seine Freunde warteten.

Als seine Füße endlich die Erde berührten, brach Timmy erleichtert zusammen.

„Danke, danke!" sagte er und schaute seine Freunde und Mrs. Figgle an.

Mrs. Figgle klopfte Timmy auf die Schulter. „Nun, junger Mann, ich hoffe, du hast heute eine wertvolle Lektion gelernt."

Timmy nickte, sein Gesicht war rot vor Verlegenheit. „Ich habe! Ich verspreche, dass ich nie wieder zu viele Süßigkeiten essen werde."

„Und denk daran," sagte Mrs. Figgle mit einem Augenzwinkern, „Magie ist am besten in Maßen zu genießen."

Die Kinder lachten alle, und Timmy, obwohl er ein wenig erschüttert war, stimmte ein. Von diesem Tag an beschränkte sich Timmy auf nur eine fliegende Süßigkeit—genau genug für ein wenig Spaß, aber nie genug, um ihn wieder in den Himmel zu schicken.

Was die magischen Süßigkeiten von Mrs. Figgle betrifft, so blieben sie das Gesprächsthema der Whizzpop Lane, und die Kinder von Muddlebrook genossen ihre sanften Schwebereisen—immer daran denkend, die Regeln zu befolgen.

Denn am Ende lernten sie alle, dass zu viel von etwas Gutem einen ein wenig zu weit vom Boden wegbringen kann!